For Ben Hur Lampman

from WILLIAM STAFFORD

In this lonely country after sundown
a big rock will stay warm
a long time. If the moon
shines that night you can see
a new version of what went on
before—shadow and light, the long
swinging caravan. It all shines deep
inside the head, warm, cold, the world.

There is in this order for thought:
its own discovery. And that is
new every day—sun, moon, the slow
changes of distance, time. You pick up
stories like these. You turn them
over and let them fall. Your whole life
could follow this even seeking and
leaving, warmed by such stories you find.

Where Would You Go?

EXPLORING THE SEASONS
with
BEN HUR LAMPMAN

Edited and With an Introduction by
V. S. HIDY

Illustrated by John Killmaster

R. O. BEATTY & ASSOCIATES • BOISE, IDAHO U.S.A.

Other books by Ben Hur Lampman

The Tramp Printer   At the End of the Car Line   The Wild Swan
How Could I Be Forgetting?   Here Comes Somebody   The Coming of the
Pondfishes   A Leaf From French Eddy

Published in the fall of 1975 by R. O. Beatty and Associates, Inc., P. O. Box 763, Boise, Idaho 83701.

Library of Congress Catalogue Card Number: 75–27433
ISBN 0–916238–01–6 paper

Printed in the United States of America

Foreword

It is sweetly fitting that this second volume of the Lampman papers should appear just in time to round out the decade. Like the first, *A Leaf From French Eddy,* this one is a gem of the purest ray serene.

That it meets this same highest of standards is due in no small measure to the sure hand of Vernon S. Hidy, the editor of both volumes. With this one, Hidy has again done for Lampman what John McDonald did for Theodore Gordon—or indeed, what Mendelssohn did for Bach—the rescue from oblivion of an otherwise surely lost masterpiece. From transient columns of yellowing and brittle newsprint he has assembled—though I would rather term it a "creative reconstruction"—a viable work of art that, but for his efforts, would never have achieved a separate existence.

This book is a unique evocation of the year's four seasons. I don't know where you would go to find its counterpart, at least in words. The only one I can think of is Vivaldi's, in the language of music. The analogy is apt, I think, because while you read these seasonal pieces in this book first for sense, you find yourself almost immediately rereading them for pleasure, like the rehearing of music that you find pleasing.

And, so much music is there in Lampman's language, on reading it again you find yourself daydreaming just as you do on hearing again a much-loved tune.

Among the "tunes" in this lyric amalgam of sense and sound, my own two favorites are the last two—perhaps partly because I hated to see the volume end. "Snow is for Country Places" seems to me the best celebration of that natural phenomenon since Whittier's "Snowbound" of more than a century ago.

And as for "A Christmas Reverie," that alone gives this book an extra dimension as something very special, for reading as well as sharing, on Christmas morning; for of all times that surely is the one time when you are better than your everyday best.

But not alone on Christmas morning, for this is a book for more than a day. Any home that has Ben Hur Lampman in it is a better home than it could otherwise ever hope to be.

ARNOLD GINGRICH

New York City
August, 1975

Contents

Introduction

As we approach our nation's 200th Birthday, Americans everywhere are appreciating more our heritage of natural beauty and our leisure to enjoy it. Today, nearly every school teaches courses related to the environment. This is an ideal time to read Ben Hur Lampman, one of America's great naturalist-philosophers and essayists, whose master works have gone almost unnoticed outside of Oregon, the state where he lived and wrote for forty years. If he were alive today, he would smile with satisfaction at the popularity of backpacking into the wilderness and the record-breaking number of visitors to our national and state parks. He spent his life savoring the trails of mountains, boating and fishing beautiful rivers and lakes, combing the beaches and writing about what he saw, what he felt and was best worth remembering. Some unforgettable pictures came out of his mellow typewriter. Who could forget *April on Sauvie Island?* . . . *Hill Water* or *A Tryst With October the Dancer?*

Lampman's writing was more sensitive and lyrical than the writings of Thoreau, Burroughs, Muir, Leopold or Krutch. All of these keen observers of nature take us to the beautiful, quiet places; but it is Lampman who, through his lyrical prose, lets us see and smell and hear and feel it all. We are right there at his side. Our heartbeat quickens as we read his rhythmic sentences. Some of his happy phrases lodge in our memory and weave themselves into our reveries through the years. . . . "a certain silence that possesses voices". . . . "the blue curvature of heaven". . . . "trout drowsing under the emerald and spume". . . . "time is the only distance".

By any measure, Ben Hur Lampman is a delightful companion at home, on trails or rivers, on weekend strolls or drives through the back-country. You may now, for the first time, carry him in your pocket or your pack. You may wish to have two copies, for you will assuredly develop a strong desire to reread certain essays from time to time; and you will want to share their inspiration and beauty with friends. Lampman is a master at staging those scenes of pure delight and joy which we find in the outdoor world around us. He is also a stylist full of surprises— a warmhearted sentimentalist with the soul of a friendly leprechaun always willing to share his treasures.

Good reading! If you appreciate the colors, the moods and the beauties of nature described by an artist with words, you are about to become a Ben Hur Lampman fan. Where will we find a more talented observer of the world in all weathers and seasons with such power to enliven the human spirit?

V. S. Hidy

V. S. HIDY

Cannon Beach, Oregon
March, 1975

You Could Look Around. . . .

Under a cloudy sky, when the woods go dim and sounds turn gray and far, you could disappear. You could look around, then step from a road through a fringe of brush, and the whole world would be a masterpiece—downed logs half returned to earth, crisscrossed limbs, and the long, dim aisles that wait for whatever waits for the world. Everything loud becomes soft and pearly as a drop of rain. A gray bird sings its one note and leads farther and farther where the trail of your life goes.

This journey, "to be far in a lonely place and yet escape loneliness," is an immediate possibility, actually, or in the pages of a book. Ben Hur Lampman has exactly touched that natural scene and its mystery. We can't tell whether our surroundings are really that way or were presented to us so congenially that author and landscape are one.

Here is the book. Step through that fringe of brush. Find this world before it disappears.

WILLIAM STAFFORD

SPRING

Where Would You Go?

A purple canyon . . . or the spray of the sea

Where would you go? With the will and way of it, and never a care for time, nor a fret for absence, and all of an eagerness, where would you go?

He said that he would go to a purple canyon, south and south of here, where of mornings the shadows are long and magical, and when you come to the creek for water the deer have been there but a moment before. And all the voices of the canyon are of the trees, and the creek, and the whistling flutter of a wild drake's wing low above the brisk current. And all the odors of the canyon are of leaf and fern, and a wetness of rocks that are liveried in moss, and the good odor of fallen trees that yield themselves to earth both graciously and gratefully. And because of this, all this, there is a certain peacefulness and healing in the purple canyon not elsewhere to be encountered.

When it is noon in the purple canyon, and the sun soars slowly over the forest and hills as a golden hawk, the rounded boulders of the creek shimmer and dance in the warmth of the sun, and on the countenance of the cliff, where every crevice has its flower in blossom, the warmth of the ancient sun is pooled for a blue lizard drowsing. There is a silence of sunshine then in the canyon, and silver and silent the trout are drowsing under the emerald and spume. How far away, and yet how near and clement, is the blue curvature of heaven. So to observe it, idling in the canyon, recumbent, drowsy, while central in the blueness a wing turns and flashes.

For when it is noon in the canyon, and the rocks are heated in the sun, the shade and shadows of the canyon are as drink from a spring in the cedars. They are vital and cool and pleasant, and in them is that property which makes of time a little thing and futile, unregarded, without purport—when it is noon in the canyon. It is an hour wherein the sun, from leaf, and frond, and flower, and water, and fallen tree, and his own excellence, distills a cordial that is peace. And those that drink of it, in the shadow of the cedar, wonder greatly but with nothing of impatience, why men have strayed from this.

There is a pagan who rouses then in the heart, with laughter of the old, forgotten deities—for the wonder of morning and the shadowed peace of noon.

Twilight comes to the canyon with bended head, wearing a lone white star, and the mystery of forests walks with her. And firelight flutters against the canyon wall, and the bird calls. Listen. Save for morning, and for noon, this is the hour of them all.

Where would you go? With time of no moment to you, and the road running swiftly to your goal, and all of an eagerness, where would you go?

He said that he would go to the sea, to the long and wonderful beaches, to taste of the wind again and to have the spray on his lips. Where the gulls scream as the wave breaks. Where the cormorant fishes. And with the wind in his face and the spray on his lips he should feel that after long exile he had come home again, and was as a boy in his mother's house. The plume of a freighter would be thinning along the skyline that is the curve of the planet, and he would drink of the scent and sound of the sea with the thirst of his necessity. And the old marvel and gladness would be in his eyes so to see her again, and a pagan, joyous and elate would rise in his heart to praise her with words that have no utterance.

How is it the sea contrives to heal and to comfort, to bring gladness out of wild and shoreless waters? And how may it be that one, to whom the sea has been stranger, stands at long last on a headland, the surf thunderous, hollow, magnificent, and over and over—thus to himself—repeats, "I have been here before. Long since. I have been here before"? How might this be?

Merely to be with the sea—so he said—were enough. So to be home again after travel. To walk with her, dream with her, wake with her, forgetting that ever there was a province beyond this. This were sufficient.

SPRING

Now there is this about the sea at morning, before the wind freshens, which weakens all phrasing. The blue vastness glinting under the sun, the level sands, the elderly outposts of rock at whose feet the tide whispers. The way of the sun with a seabird that rises above the curve of a breaker, down which the white, white foam is spun. The measured, meditative, timeless repetition of the returning tide. And that elixir, formed of wave and sea-growth, and of the excellent sun, which comes with healing on the breath of the sea–that memorable, ageless, wild fragrance which is the breathing of the sea.

But whether it is at morning, or noon, or evening or starlight, the sea is refuge and healing, and if the sea is roused by storm this also transmits strength to those who observe it, testing the spume of the sea, and marveling as children might at her incomparable strength and majesty. At all times the sight of the sea, to one who has been away, rouses a marveling and a gladness in his eyes, and wakes the pagan in his heart. And there are words that have no utterance.

Where would you go? With the will and the way of it, and time of small account, and not a care for absence, and the road waiting, where would you go?

April On Sauvie Island

Spices and jewels at Big Sturgeon

The wild currant is blooming—said the Old Copy Reader—where it has something of shelter. Now there is a color I defy them to copy. It is for April's brush and not one of ours. They do very well with roses, but the wild currant is somewhat beyond them. For the wild currant is a mood of April and only April may paint it. But that is aside from what I was about to tell you.

What I was about to tell you was not about the wild currant but about the way the willows are leafing. It is a positive excitement. When a willow leaf swells from the twig, in a long slender bud eager to open, the leaf is enclosed in a substance that sticks to the fingers as varnish might, and, indeed, the bud appears to have been varnished. It is in the odor of this vernal substance that I have my greatest delight. So one of the old-time spice ships may have enlivened the wind, long ago and far away, if its cargo was especially fortunate. Where there are many willows, and chiefly in the river bottoms now, the spiced breathing of the willow buds is as fine as the singing of redwings. As for myself, I never can breathe a sufficiency of it.

And high over the willows, hugely against the drifting clouds and the blueness, and the dark shower, the mated ospreys were perched. They are gigantic birds that have the seeming of eagles. And earnestly I pray that nobody may come upon them with a gun to do them scathe, but if by chance he should, then may his aim be shaken by desire. They lifted heavily from time to time and played above the waking cottonwoods, the oaks and the ash. Somehow it seemed to me that but for the excitement of the willow scent the ospreys never would have been there for our discovery. The doomed golden carp, these swam in the windless, sheltered water.

I wish you might have been there—said the Old Copy Reader—to see those fish hawks wheel and fondly harry one another. Unless they come to harm doubtless they'll nest nearby. But, Lord, that wasn't all of it! The wood ducks, they were fairly everywhere, the drakes like plumed jewels, such as the people of Mexico fashioned with their most ancient and exquisite arts. The wood ducks were flying everywhere across the bottoms, crying with that half-wistful plover-call of theirs. And we, in the scent of the willows, know an ache that is ancient as spring—an ache that is gladness and something else.

All the long morning the geese were in flight, and their V's came clamorously out of the north, where the river is, and over the cotton-woods, company after company. There were not many birds in each flight, not more than fifty in the largest, likely, but the succession of them seemed interminable, and I suppose we must have seen a thousand or more of geese. They were going in to Big Sturgeon Lake, like always when it is April, and you couldn't mistake their gladness in the day. They were as glad as we.

Well, sir, there was a turtle on nearly every log, but so evil is our reputation, sir, so quite notorious, that never a turtle of them all would wait until we might draw near and give him greeting. They lifted their heads in still carvings, motionlessly vigilant, while yet we were a long way off, and when we had passed some invisible deadline known well to turtles they returned to the water. It was admirably done. Though turtles

April On Sauvie Island

cannot leap they have a practice for such occasions. They simply tumble off the log, and so are seen no more—unless it be that one of the boldest ventures the tip of his nose to see if you are yet nearby. And if you are, he draws it underneath the surface and waves his heavy limbs and darkly sinks. When all the air was spiced with the willow-smell, and the wood ducks were calling, the wild geese bugling, it seemed a grievous thing to us that turtles would not trust our mood of innocence.

There was a minor serpent on a bit of floating driftwood, midway of the yellow water, and he was jade and lacquer, most exquisitely fashioned —tranced by his own sorcery—lifeless and timeless quiet—until we came too near. Then the small serpent, remembering Eden, would not trust us nearer. It made a silver course toward the shore, and our strange prayers, that followed the serpent tensely, perhaps preserved it. For no bass rose to seize it. And thus it entered the willows glintingly, where they wade, and it was gone. Should ever you chance upon a small striped snake in that vicinity, a serpent of lacquer and of jade, withhold your cudgel, I charge you. It is mine.

Ospreys, wood ducks, wild geese, the awkward turtles, painted, the lacquered serpent, the very pattern of the shower on the water, the heavy rising of the golden carp—all these are mine. Yes, and the breathing of the willows when they are ready to put forth their leaves, in April when the wild currant is blooming on Sauvie Island.

Hill Trail

A mystery by a tumbledown cabin

They said, "Nobody has been in there yet this year," and he turned his face to the hills. For a matter of miles the trail was evident enough, but at length it became difficult with fern, and not until the wild steepness of it led him to the ridge, was he confident that he had kept the way. There the trail was evident again, though without sign of recent use, and he paused to drink of the hill wind, for it had been a long climb.

"Someone waited here not long ago," he thought, and laughed at this absurdity. It couldn't be. And yet he felt, somehow, that it had not been long ago. There were yellow mimulus flowers in the rock crevices and a stillness in which were the conversations of the trees. He listened with an intenseness that mocked him, and searched the slope of the ridge that plunges, in strewn stone, down to the heavy, dark forest again.

"Someone passed this way within the hour," he thought, and knew this could not have been. For they had told him, and he knew, that none had been there before him.

Yet someone had paused there, so he would have vowed, that very morning, and had turned to see the blue thread of the river, touched with silver, remotely down and distant; had marked, as he did, how the massive and heroic hills from that vantage became smooth and flowing and gentle of line—had loved it all, the hills, the hill wind and the stillness, and had entered the canyon and the renewed forest down that same trail. Yet none had been there they said.

He found himself searching the slope again, as though he might see this predecessor, and for a long moment scrutinized the boulder, halfway to the thicket, that might have been someone at ease beneath a fir. There was a feeling of companionship and of fraternity that would not be denied. But they had been so positive about it. No one had been there.

The way down to the canyon was more difficult than had been the ascent to the ridge, for it fell sharply over the upper slope and entered the trees again by a declivity that necessitated the grasping of roots and boughs as he descended. The dew was yet on the brush he parted, the fern was undisturbed, and his feet felt hither and yon for the trail he could not see. He marked the tall great tree beneath him, for they had spoken of this guidance, where he would turn to the left hand and so avoid the cliff.

"Someone will be there surely," he thought. A grouse flushed at his feet. His hands were torn by briars. "This trail has not been used since late last summer," he reflected. And yet, oddly, there was an assurance that someone would be resting at the foot of the great spruce.

For a score of yards or so, as one nears the spruce, the undergrowth falls back as though in tribute and the trail is plain again. It is there that deer are sometimes seen, and in the black dampness of the trail a cougar may have left his pad-print. He pressed the tangle aside and entered the opening, with the sunshine flooding it, but at the foot of the spruce no one awaited. He smiled at himself as he searched for sign of a previous presence. None had been there. And yet. . . .

Hill Trail

So, for the space of a pipe, he rested again, and listened, and laughed aloud at the whimsy of it—and the forest made of his laughter a sound strange to him, and impious, and the stillness succeeded. Deer had walked in the trail, and lately, but there were no prints of leather and hob-nails.

Over and over, wordlessly, the silence repeated that someone had been there within the hour. And he rose to his feet again. It should be half a mile, and not more, to the creek and the tumbledown cabin the homesteaders built there. Rough going. "Whoever has been here," he thought, "will camp at the cabin." But that could not be.

So he came to the grooved floor of the canyon, and the creek in its shallow, with the deep swirling pool just below, and the clearing beyond,

SPRING

and the tumbledown cabin—but on the sand by the ford there were no bootprints. The sand lay level and unmarred as the last rain had left it. This was as it should have been, and yet it was of a strange unnaturalness. Blue jays were quarreling in the alders and the drumming of a grouse echoed his heart-beats in the sunny silence. He waded the creek and pressed through the grass to the cabin, and with something of eagerness. It was untenanted, as he had known it would be, and the ashes on its hearth were sodden with the dampness of months.

"Of course," he said to himself, "for they told me that nobody had been here yet this year."

Yet somebody stood in the doorway, he felt, no longer than an hour since, and looked toward the creek and the pool, and the steepness of the forest that lifts to the ridge on the top of the world—surely somebody stood there, while the tiredness quitted him also, and it was good to be weary.

He called from the doorway, as woodsmen and fishermen call to each other, and the cliff alone gave it back to him.

"First of all," he thought, "I shall make coffee."

Up Schooner Creek

Thigh-deep in hill water

We have received, in a letter just opened, an invitation to go fishing—up Schooner creek. It is an unusual proposal in that the fisherman who makes it cannot visit the pool we both have in mind, and knows as well that we, too, are restrained. The correspondent is remote from Schooner creek, and is moreover engaged in duties that admit of no departure.

Nevertheless, here is the letter, and it suggests that, without quitting our respective desks, we, too, may revisit the coolness where water ouzels are singing. At least, so it would seem, they should be singing at this season of the year. What is the way a cedar has with the wind, and what is a cedar saying? You who have listened to cedars, and firs, and spruces that grow on hillsides lifting up from creeks—it is you who may answer, if you have found the words for it. The lost words that escape the tongue, but which are memorable to the spirit.

Up Schooner creek, and into the grave and whispering stillness that is so singularly happy and elate. There are few farms in the deep valley. They are far between, and it is such a region as the deer attest with their hoof marks, daintily in the clay. Few farms and restful, and nothing much of a road. When this green country was planned, range and woodland meadow, crest and slope, there were certain provisions for the refreshment we have named water. The mists are restored to the sea, the southwest rains go home again, in a brightness of rivers and creeks. Thus it was ordered. And the redtail hawk, swinging in great circles above the forest, sees Schooner creek where it journeys, and the twisting road that attends this pilgrimage. You have on Schooner creek a certain silence that possesses voices, gently suited to silence, and you have peace. And healing. Lift up your faces to the cedars. They also know the fleeting, curious, wonderful gift that is called life. The air is damp with fern.

The correspondent has declared that we must fish a certain pool, or eddy, or reflective loitering—where willows drink and the alders are splotched with mosses, and where white clover creeps down to the margin and columbine has paused. There is the passing shadow of wings on the blossomed clover, and wild pigeons are calling. What is it that we fish for with our lures and baits? What manner of trout can it be that we desire to capture? It were vain to declare the purpose, for the purpose flashes and recedes, as a fish that has risen. For time beyond reckoning men have fished such pools as this, and though they have taken many fishes, and mourned the loss of not a few, deep down within them—deeper far than any loitering of waters, where Schooner creek dreams of the sea—they understand that it is but clouds they catch, and the conversations of birds, and the fragrance of fern, and something else that eludes definition. The pursued. The pursuing. That which is taken and yet lost. Are there dryads in the alders and can it be that creeks have character and sentience?

We have fished the pool, and seven trout are lustrous against the wet marsh-grasses. Up Schooner creek, and we have come to the canyon that is not often fished, because of its steepness, and also because in the depths of it the creek repeatedly is barricaded with the lost trees of winter freshets. Yet here is good fishing, and not infrequently the turning flank, the silver instancy, of such a trout as fishermen have pondered when they

were distant from streams. It is a goodly canyon, and comfortable, if taken in leisurely fashion, without undue haste, with all regard for the shadow and shouting and marvel of it. You must prepare for at least two hours of clambering, and of wading thigh-deep in hill water, if you would fish the canyon. But you will be repaid. Up Schooner creek.

By trout? Is it that you anticipate such settlement as this? We have no more than twenty fish, it may be, in the creels—against wet grass and fronds of bracken—but we must look more closely. They are not trout you count, not wholly, when you have fished a hill creek. And if you do not understand the meaning of this, then surely you have never fished such a stream. Yes, it is certain as aught may be that you have never been up Schooner creek along about this time of the year.

The Song Of Wings

Flowing and weaving against the sky

All along the taut wire, darkly beaded along the silver tenseness, the swallows were waiting a wind. Under them the black road ran, and the willows swept away to the river, where the river moves gravely toward an end of rivers. And over them the shaping, softly restless clouds, figures of mist and dream.

Over them, too, their sun—the swallow's sun, that is kindled for the warmth of swallows, for the contentment of swallows, and for the way it has with a feather. Red cow, deep in the rushes, monstrous and laggard, dull and slothful, what do you know of the sun, and the wind, and the face of the river? You who are earthbound? Little gray rabbit, small drabness in the clover, crouched, fearful—what can you know of wings and the wind on the water? Of the way of a sun with a feather? Then all the swallows moved their wings somewhat, stirring slightly, and movement fled along the swallows as a word passes. They were motionless on the silver tenseness, waiting for the wind. Would the wind come? It would come. For this is a swallow's world.

The cottonwoods told it first—the tall and slender cottonwoods that watch beside the river, drinking of the river, whispering to the river, thinking the river to be theirs. "Here is wind!" said the leaves where the little brown falcon perches. Whispering that there was wind. "Here is wind!" said the leaves of the branches where nests are hidden. Whispering that wind was walking inland from the sea. "Here is wind!" said the leaves that look down upon a small tree-frog, a bronze and emerald tree-frog, singing to himself. Over and over. Endlessly repeating. "It is the wind!" exclaimed all the cottonwoods, and they flashed their leaves to the hand of the wind, and the wind went among them like a voice. The willows were whispering, too—but the cottonwoods told it first. The river, all of a moment, was penciled and fretted, where the river seemed to flow inland because the wind was coming. Ho, wind! There the wind came like laughter.

Along the taut wire, the silver tenseness of it, the dark and beaded swallows woke to fire. They stirred and were smitten with flame. They lifted their wings and the sun had its way with them. They lifted their wings as song begins, and the wind took them, and they were kin to the wind. Weaving, flowing, going, returning, glinting, curving, they wrought the pattern of the swallows, the ageless weave and fabric of the swallows, against tree and river and sky. They were more fleet than leaves that are blown. They were impermanent and changing as dream.

The Song Of Wings

21

Not the stroke of a sword, the flash of a spear, the voice of the thrush—nor aught that is seen, or heard, or touched with fingers or felt within the heart—makes song as the swallows made it, silently, when they drew the song of the swallows over the flow of the stream, while the wind walked. You who are earth-bound, you in the hazel, you in the sedges and you on the black road that fares nowhere—it is a swallow's world!

A River Near To The Sea

Secret . . . lingering . . . content with loneliness

The west wind cannot come at this river, because the dark water is of many windings and also because—until the river enters the marshes of the bay—it is defined and sheltered by those alders and willows that love it well. The west wind cannot come at it and all its lower reaches under the alders are smooth as the cheek of a child, but nevertheless are of a burnished, dreaming darkness. It has a secret place, this secret water, and it is well content with loneliness. Secret upon the river, sheltered by its own alders, one hears the surf and the surges, the white sea to westward, drowsily as a drowsy voice—reiterant, slumbrous.

On yesterday all this was mountain water, born of the veins of the hills, where an eagle has her eyrie and men have lately seen three elk. On yesterday. Then it was hasty water, laced and ribboned with spray, that carved at the hills of origin and made a song to the hills. Then it was green and undulant water, rhythmic with urgency, as it swept to the rock that should part it—the rock that lifts and strives in the canyon as a plow in wild, strange loam. Yesterday. Then it was clear and cheerful water, shallow with warmth, and the dwarfish small sculpins, the banded trout parr, played and sunned and slew in its shallows. Where men have seen three elk and the one antlered. On yesterday.

So much of haste and of whiteness, old as time, young as the moment, to come at long last to a secret place of alders and willows, not far from the marshes—and to be tinctured by the tide and to linger before the sea. You might say, if you were pagan, that the stream is remembering and that it is hesitant only for recollection before it is one with the sea and so is lost to the hills. Eager on yesterday, yet now without fear, without reluctance, thinking of cedars and canyons before the sea has it. Meditative and dreaming in a secret place, where the sound of the sea is softened. The salt tides.

It is there the mergansers are fishing and the pates of the drakes are flame in the mottled sunlight. There is a boat at the shore and the tides have written it over with decay. In the slow eddy, whose waters are darkly golden, there are leaves that dance very gravely and a trout rising. And a lost tree that the freshet fetched. And in the clay of the margin the otter has left her prints. This is a water that takes thought, remembering its hills, remembering yesterday, before it fares utterly beyond the dunes, with the gulls leading.

One Of The Rhoten Boys

Adventure, riddles and gold

Down southern Oregon way they are called "the Rhoten boys"— though they have been gray these many years. And Enos, so a Medford dispatch tells, has given up pocket hunting for keeps. Enos is dead. They were famous pocket hunters, all the Rhoten boys, with an uncanny knowledge of where gold could be found. They read the tumbled, rugged serial of hills and mountains, all around the Rogue river as other men would read a book. When they found a pocket, a good pocket, they spent the gold as though some fairy godmother had given it to them. It was always easy come, easy go—with the Rhoten boys. They might have been rich, and they were—a half dozen times—but they preferred to hunt pockets.

A pocket, of course, isn't a mine. It is precisely what the noun implies —a pocket. But to a pocket hunter there is more of adventure and romance—though he'd laugh to hear you phrase it that way—in the hunting of pockets than in any other pursuit of the yellow metal. There's a greater gamble. There's more of a chance. When you find a pocket it's like picking up a royal flush; the gold is there—self-evident, heavy, plastered thickly in the rotten quartz. All you have to do is to begin at the bottom of the mountain, having judged the slope of her shrewdly, and pan your way slowly up the face. For the pocket will, through many centuries, have sprinkled the slope thinly with the golden flakes. And this is the trace. You follow it, follow it, follow it—and then it may chance that you will lose it. But it may be that you will run the riddle to its source—and there's the gold, waiting, like a treasure that had been kept in trust for you since the very beginning of terrestrial time. Easy come, easy go. The Rhotens have struck it again!

SPRING

A Rhoten in the hereafter—one of those Rhoten boys? He'd be sizing up the mountains of God with the practiced eye of the born pocket hunter. And he ought to be young again—young as he was when they came to the southern Oregon country a long while ago. He'd be all of a quiet fever to go where the hawk is wheeling, if there are hawks in the hereafter. And it ought to be in the early spring of the year, always.

SUMMER

Down A Country Road

Sweetbrier and murmurous trees

There is a pleasure in reflecting that, however loud our highways may become with traffic, the country roads shall remain as lanes of comparative quietude, leading to dustless fields and thickets. Few travel them, though they are graveled, and these are only the people that dwell beside the country roads, and such others as are more than agreeable to an exchange of haste and gas fumes for leisure and the untainted atmosphere of the rural byways. To quit the highway for such a modest thoroughfare —the highway with its insistence on hurry and its too importunate eagerness—is something like turning aside, when the sun is fretful, to rest awhile in the shade of an oak.

In a few hundred yards of progress, in a quarter of a mile, the fretfulness of the highway seems an experience of long ago, fortunately past, and dimming into forgetfulness. Because the country road is lonely it manifests a curious, quiet pleasure that you have chosen it, and foxglove and sweetbrier at either hand draw near; seem then to tarry, and are gone. Birds that do not frequent the vicinage of well-traveled highways are numerous and unafraid along the country road. The air is blended of wetness, and shade, and sun, and the suspiration of solemn, murmurous trees, and of thickets where the grouse has her brood.

The times are impatient with such thoroughfares as this, for gravel is only a makeshift. Moreover, the country road wanders as it will, taking no account of the minutes that might be saved. It follows the course the wagons traveled, no doubt, when hill-springs were avoided because of the marshy wildness about them where the jewelweed trembles on its stem, and plodding around the rise was simpler and better for the horses than to drive over. If there arose a great outcropping of stone before them, dark with seepage from the wild hillsides, the delicate fronds of maidenhair fern at its base, why the horses went around. It was simpler so. And since to this day such roads are of little account, when the imperative, swift flow of traffic is dwelt upon, they remain as they were save for a trifle of grading and gravel, and it seems best for quite another reason.

These are the roads that lead away from the signboards and paints of the highway, into a province that does not tempt the commercial. You will say that, at a distance of seven miles or so, the country road comes again to a highway, as a creek to its river, and so is lost. Well, seven miles are seven miles, and meantime the country road seems to curve and loiter, most agreeably, through an inheritance we had not thought to recover.

Smith's Road, Cupper Road, Rock Creek Road, Four Mile Road, Pleasant Hollow Road—they'll not be paved these years and years to come. It wouldn't be profitable. And they lead to nowhere. There is more truth in this than the engineers may imagine. For it wouldn't be profitable—that is true. Improve them by straightening the curves, and shattering the rock where the maidenhair fern is cool, and tiling the spring where the jewelweed blossoms, and cutting away the hillside that at this season is terraced with the tall foxglove? No, they are wholly right about the matter. It wouldn't be profitable, though a dozen clamorous billboards were standing at the bend.

The Water Of The Hills

Icy and delicate blue

As summer advances a great many of us are becoming thirsty for hill water. This is a restlessness not otherwise to be remedied. For you will fall to thinking of places you have known in the grave and friendly forest, where small, clear streams ran with light laughter across the trail, and you set your knees to the wet, bright pebbles and stooped to drink. Or it may have been a spring in the fern with the black loam of the forest exposed by the hooves of deer that had refreshed themselves. Such water is chill from the calmness of earth, and rock, and shadow. It is newly released from the secret veins of her, and a delicate blueness suffuses it, as though a mist were prisoned in the pool. It is not difficult to fancy oneself again the pagan, as one kneels there, for a curious, friendly imminence of enchantment, of charmed quietude, presses close. Listen. It is only the wind in the cedar.

The bright chillness of a mountain spring or hill stream is scarcely believable, as it is told, save by the initiate. The clarity of the water is such that a pool which appears no more than a foot or so in depth, so sharply etched and evident are its pebbles, may in simple fact be six or seven feet deep. So chill is the water that he who drinks would vow it has been newly iced—which approximates the truth. Such is the origin of all our rivers you might say, and not be wide from the circumstance—the little streams and great. Is it not to be marveled at that the small trout which frequent our mountain streams are brave as they are beautiful?

To give thanks for thirst is to yield a deep and primal gratitude to the providence that arranged this place and made provision for the deer, for the quail, for the wood mouse, for the brown wild rabbit with gentle eyes of fear, and for the wayfarer who cannot quite forget that once upon a time, and ever so long ago, the forest was his dwelling. There is nothing of taint nor of evil in this cup. It is worth, truly and of itself, the miles that have been put behind—the miles that have left the valley at a great distance, with a thread of saffron road winding down it. To give thanks for thirst.

Whoever drinks of hill water is taking memory into his heart. For so long a time as remains to him, wherever he may chance to be, there shall return the memory of that place—to give him thirst again. The thirst for trees that are untamed and ancient. For shadow and silence that seem always to have been. For the long cathedral lights the sun contrives, slantingly through the firs. For the song of the cedar when the wind is from the sea. For the muted voices of the forest. For the new, chill water of his well-remembered hills. Of such nature must be his thirst who takes this memory into his heart.

There is a spring by a hill to westward, and evening comes out of the canyon as a presence, gracious and cool, to summon a star to the crest of the mountain, and fashion vapors for the young river. The cabin is old and forsaken, for men have quitted the place, and the wild hay grows in the meadow, and the deer will come to it at twilight and dawn. And to the left hand, toward evening and the presence of evening, you may follow the weathered rails to the spring.

Drink deeply. You will be taking memory into your heart.

Why There Are Water Lilies There

A gesture out of the heart

This is a simple story and soon told, by way of explaining how the white and seashell waterlilies came to be—for never did they chance—in the little cupped dune lake back of beyond. So you are warned of its simplicity, and need not read on if you are one who has a taste for plot. And what is plot, for that matter, but an interweaving of the simplicities? And simple things comprise this complex experience we pilgrims have called living.

It may be that some day you will cross the Oregon dunes, the tawny silence of them, the pale golden immensity, to find the lake beyond. If it is summer then, as properly it should be, and the rhododendron long blossomed, and the scarlet salmon berries in fruit, there will be water-lilies, both white and pink, opened to the sun in a mirrored cove of the secret lake that is hidden there. Now who can it have been that planted the waterlilies there, for such blossoms are in nowise native? Ours is the yellow pond lily, the spatterdock—but these come from far.

The boat will breast nearer and nearer, to the cove where the scented great blossoms are floating, sustained by their islands of leaves, beneath which the bass hide away for long contemplation. The boat will rest there by that scented strangeness, the oars dripping. If it is you who have found the waterlilies in the mirrored cove, do not pick one. They tire so soon, and all their beauty is withered when they are taken away.

And you will be right—these did come from far. These flowers came from the distance of time, out of the memory of time, and there is a distance, so fondly near, so very remote, as to challenge all measurement. For a thousand miles, or multiple thousands, as distance is measured, may soon be spanned. But for the distance that is named time, once you have put it behind you, there is no fleetness which may traverse it. The waterlilies of the lake beyond the dunes were, in truth, planted there in defiance of time; which is a gesture—out of the heart—that we call sentiment. And a brave gesture it is, and itself the meaning of living. These waterlilies came from fifty years ago. They came from a summer day in Iowa, in the year of '86. That is why they are where you will find them.

On that agreeable morning, with the wind in the corn, and the bay mare in harness, and illimitable time, as it seemed, beckoning on and on like the country road, they drove in the red-wheeled buggy across the pleasant day. There were all manner of birds in the wayside tangle, redwings and larkspurs, and blackbirds with yellow bonnets. And there were sooty tern in the ditches, and the whistle and winnow of waterfowl wings. The last of the sweetbrier was blossoming.

And they were dressed in their Sunday best, those two—they would seem quaint to us now, and more than rural. Oh, white flounces, one supposes, and perhaps an elegant silken parasol, and the high buttoned shoes whose tops were demurely hidden by the long skirt. And he in heavy serge, double-breasted perhaps, or with coattail curved and abbreviated, and what then was known as a stand-up collar, and clattering cuffs and a bow necktie secured by a band of elastic, or by a cunning device that anchored it, theoretically, to a tarnished collar-button. And tan shoes with toothpick toes. And he probably wore a derby hat, with perhaps a small dent in it.

Whip-tassel flying in the country air. Get along, Nellie! To the little bay mare. Time was a country road, stretching before them, illimitably, amusingly, thrillingly, with never an end to it. They heard, without hearing, the trilling of the cranes. Clop-clop. Clop-clop. Go on Nellie. And they laughed at little or nothing, and laughter went with them. Time was a country road.

So they sped past—you must not smile at the phrasing—the Stebbins place with its vast red barn, and shining cattle, and they spoke of the crop the Stebbinses surely would harvest. A rabbit rushed out of the sweetbrier and would have escaped in fleet terror, but there was no harm in them. The rabbit sat brownly, meditatively, by the roadside and watched them go past, driving the little bay mare. All the fields, the groves, the sweep of the prairie, were gently sorcerous then—were touched

by an enchantment they did not trouble to name. And they passed by Peterson's place, and they waved to him at the well. And the wheels of the buggy drummed and rattled the loose planks of the bridge across Lime creek.

"Waterlilies!" she cried. You know—the shrillness, exclamatory, exciting, and eager, yet musical, too. Yes, that is well said. It is like music. "Waterlilies!" She exclaimed again, half rising to see.

And "Whoa!" said the tall boy beside her. "Whoa, Nellie!" The little bay mare stopped agreeably, and turned her sleek head to look inquiringly at them. And then, for there was no check-rein, took a step forward and bent to the wayside clover. The two of them sat there, in a bright stillness of which, the world over, they were the only inhabitants. They sat there and looked at the cove that was formed by the bend of Lime creek.

Beyond the sedges and cattails, lightly stirring to the west wind, the sheltered and musing water was open, and teal moved among the white waterlilies at the right-hand.

"I love them so," the girl said.

The boy looped the reins around the whipstalk, for the bay mare would stand without hitching, and sprang out of the buggy. And he smiled at the girl, and he looked at the water, and as he advanced upon the cove of Lime creek he heard the voices of heroes and the songs of troubadours that were dust these many centuries, and into the marshy margin he went without hesitation.

"You musn't!" she called to him. But he was committed to the adventure, toothpick tan shoes, Sunday suit and all, and he floundered resolutely on through the cattail. The ooze of an Iowa cove is reluctant material. Reckless of sleeve or cuff he stooped to the lilies, white and golden on the dark water—and he brought them back with long stems, as he must. He fetched back seven waterlilies, and it was worth the endeavor.

Fifty long, fleet, brief, laggard years ago—when time was a country road. Back In Iowa. That is why there are waterlilies now, white ones and pink ones, in a dune lake in Oregon.

Time is the only distance.

The Sea Belongs To The Sandpipers

Unperturbed by spindrift and smother

The elemental forces of the sea contrived a green great wave far offshore, far from the swept and sloping sands, and sent it hurrying landward over the valleys of ocean. And toweringly it grew until the surf-ducks took refuge in the jade heart of it and all its crest was torn with spindrift, and whiteness raced its length as though the wave tossed a wild, white mane to see the shore. The wave fell thunderously in a broken wildness of water, and from the smother of its fall was sped the last impulse of the wave. The sands received it where the sandpipers were gleaning. "The sea has sent a wave to us," said the sandpipers voicelessly, and they wheeled as one bird and ran before the spent foam of that tired surf, yet gleaning as they ran. The sea seemed reaching for them.

Be of good cheer about this matter, however. The sea never will capture one of the sandpiper folk, that have their home between the sea and the drift. For if the wash of the wave comes nearer to them than the length of a sandpiper's stride, which is a pathetic but quite effective absurdity, the rear flank, never glancing at the sea, flutters cheerfully forward above the pattering companions and becomes the van. The sandpipers glean right and left, unperturbed, and they wheel as a squadron of lancers might wheel when the spent water retreats, and follow it down to the shale. Are there, indeed, generals of sandpipers? Brigadiers? Field marshals? They have wheeled again and are hastening up the sloping sands, gleaning as they come, with the tired surf whispering almost at their shanks. The rear rank flutters forward. Give over this endeavor, ocean. You shall not capture a sandpiper this day, nor ever.

And that is one point of view; but the other, and quite the more reasonable, too, is the opinion of the sandpiper folk on this matter. For

they know—or they should if they troubled to give the least reflection to things that were determined long since—they know the sea for their patroness and friend, and that her beaches are theirs for the gleaning, and that always she prepares provision for sandpipers. For this is what all the sandpipers know, with the sea at their heels—have sandpipers heels?— or wheeling to follow the spent surf back to the tide. They know the purpose of the ocean.

She shapes a green great wave at the skyline, where the smoke of the freighter thins, or beyond the curve of the world, that her sandpipers, far and far on the sands, may be nourished. The wave comes to land with that praiseworthy purpose, the sandpipers say, and crashes in spindrift and smother. It is reasonably and manifestly a sandpiper's ocean, providentially arranged for the sandpipers, and so, why bother about it?

"The sea has sent a wave to us," said all the sandpipers voicelessly, and the wave fell thunderously.

A Handful Of Blackberries

With a cedar-bird and a cow

On indolent, sun-drenched summer afternoons, out in Suburbia, the children search the hedges and fence corners for wild blackberries, and startle the gaudy pheasants from their hiding. There is no sweetness to compare with this. There is a savor of sun in the fruit, of sun and of freedom, and time is of small account.

So the Old Copy Reader said, as he borrowed a cigarette, and glanced at his watch apprehensively, yet wearily, too.

A very great while ago—said the Old Copy Reader—beside a marsh that must long since have been ditched and tiled and drained for a field men do not need, I picked a handful of wild blackberries. There was somewhere a ruffed grouse drumming in the maples, and you could drink the gentle, small wind like water. Now I have picked many the handful of wild blackberries since that day, but that handful, above all, was memorable. Indeed, they will have drained the marsh—sighed the Old Copy Reader—for I know them well, since I am one of them myself. And a dozen of reedy acres where the redwings sing and make their nests, and the muskrat traces a silver V on the drowsy bright stillness—a place where wild blackberries come for refreshment—would seem to them of little account in its peaceful, healing freedom. They wouldn't be happy until they had ditched it—nor would they be happy then.

A Handful Of Blackberries

I picked a handful of ripe wild blackberries there, and let them dissolve on my tongue, and in so doing I made it my fate that never afterward should any fruit have half so much delight, nor any day be endowed with wonder comparable. How can I express to you the vitality and wistfulness of that simple memory, which reconstructs a time it cannot ever restore? I saw the illimitable years across the sleeping marsh, and the rushes were not more green and golden—I saw them vaguely yet confidently, and I suppose now that this was only because I experienced happiness as birds and muskrats do.

If I were a prayerful man—said the old Copy Reader—I should petition heaven that we might always keep our early illusions. For it seems now to me that there was more of saving truth in them than ever I have found in hard and undeniable fact—but I have lost the one and must accept the other.

Take me as I am now—he continued—and consider how it is with me. In a little less than the quarter of an hour, if this watch is right about it, I have to go on shift. And all the wild blackberries that ever were picked could not alter this obligation. I am bound to conform to it.

Yet that day I ate the wild blackberries beside the swamp, I had been sent to discover and drive home an errant cow that was forever straying—a black-and-white cow with a look of maiden innocence which considerably belied her true nature. It was an urgent mission, and though I departed without enthusiasm I could not but realize that others felt deeply the imperative nature of my trust. But I came across the wild blackberries—there was only one vine of them—and they glistened darkly in their plumpness and, well, you know how it is with me. Mark this well now, when you yield to temptation be as certain as is possible that you will not subsequently regret your weakness. For in this there is strength. I have never regretted pausing there by the swamp in the maples.

They melted away on my tongue—said the Old Copy Reader—and very strangely but positively I knew at once that finding the cow didn't matter so much as they thought. Not nearly so much. It was something that well could wait upon convenience and fortune. For I had been too severely impressed by the weight of my mission, until then, to hear the redwings in the rushes, or to watch the muskrat swimming across the swamp. But at the very taste of that wild, sun-blessed fruit I heard the redwings and saw the muskrat, and an awareness of the relative unimportance of anything else seeped pleasantly into my spirit. I had found the truth—though I was to lose it later, yes, even to deny it.

Near to the blackberry vine, in the cool heart of the shrub, was a cedar-bird nesting. I turned to find her looking at me, but with nothing of fear. And she accepted four berries from my hand, there on her nest, which circumstance seemed then to me to be of much greater benefit to the giver than to the brooding bird. And it seemed to me also that to give four wild blackberries to a maternal cedar-bird was surely of greater moment, and would be so recorded somewhere, than to find the black-and-white cow and hurry her home within the hour. There was waywardness in those berries, I tell you; there was something sanely rebellious. Why, of course. There was truth. If they scolded me afterward for failure, or for loitering, what matter? For I would be right about it all, and they would be wrong—and it is never wholly unpleasant to be cruelly misunderstood. Well, I got home at sunset, when most of the chores were done —and they were all prepared to misunderstand me. In fact, they did.

Did I bring home the cow?—repeated the Old Copy Reader. I'd like to tell you that the day was perfect to its close, and that I did not find the cow. But I suppose I did. The effect of that handful of wild blackberries began to wear off in the middle of the afternoon, and I had not such conviction of truth as at first I experienced. You see, I was beginning already to conform, and so to abandon certain principles that have much to do with our happiness. I was beginning to deny the truth and to acknowledge the authority of time—a most tyrannous fellow. Yes— I suppose I brought home the cow.

And these children that I see picking wild blackberries out on the fringe of the town—none knows better than I what they really are picking, though they, too, will know it some day.

On Revisiting A Very Friendly River

For the thirst of the spirit . . . the veins of a planet

There comes to this desk a letter from one who wishes that she might have her river restored to her—the river from which she is so far removed, and from which she has been so long separated. And the wish? A strange fancy, you say. Nay, the wish itself is her answer, for it is in earnest that the river flows through her heart, even now, as a stream may water a thirsty land. They that have had rivers in their times, the sweet flow of them, the laughter and the clamor, the sedate serenity, have these rivers always, forever and forever. It is so stipulated in the bond.

Yet one wishes for rivers. There is a thirst for rivers that is like to the hunger for the sea—and the thirst is not physical. You will say to yourself, "It is a comely land and agreeable." But if you search this opinion to its source, you shall find its beginning in a pleasant water, and more often in a river or its affluent, with herons set for sentinel, and wild fowl working silver patterns on the brightness of it. In rivers. More often than otherwise, in rivers. And without these the rich land would be fearsome and forbidding—to be looked upon with awe, perhaps, but never with sure and prompt affection, or not often. For rivers are life itself. They are the full and vital veins of a planet that otherwise would be waste and desolate. But rivers are as much for the thirst of the spirit as for the thirst of the sod.

Oh, surely, I know. That is to say, I know how it is with such as wish for their rivers, the rising breeze, the waking dawn, the shimmering cottonwoods, the gray lady alders, the widening circles where a trout has risen. The misty breath of them, their revealed secrecy of bend and bluff, the odor of their margins, where death is life reborn of an ancient and fathomless chemistry.

So it is, with the tide—providence favoring—running strongly inland, the gulls circling, screaming, I will come some day, and soon, to my river, and look upon the width and flow and strength of it as upon the countenance of a friend. And the tide and I will go inland, past the old cannery, past the slouching, moss-roofed farms, beyond the rock of sorcery where nets are spread for salmon—inland and inland to a pool I know. The river, the tide, and myself—as it was in the beginning.

People that frequent rivers have many signboards, and these are undefaced. There are trees that tell how far it will be to such a bend or landing. There are weathered snags, fixed firmly in the silt and sand, that indicate the miles—let us say—to Scott's place or the Drift creek trail. And the unfolding hills have tongues of silence, wherewith to name the way. All this is as it should be, and is well bethought—for the river has been a thoroughfare for a great length of time. Century upon century.

There's a creek comes down from the ranges to shape a pool in the river, by permission of the river, and all day long the pool is guarded most watchfully by the shadow that never quits it—the shadow of the range. And all day long the pool turns upon itself, in a dark witchery, with leaves that spin and loiter; and all the long day the pool is fretted and broken by the rising of the fish that dwell there. With a white farm to the right hand, and the green forest to the left. And a certain peace that is not elsewhere to be bartered for nor bought. And the time shall be hours, and the hours shall be both laggard and fleet.

And, after a while, we will fare yet inland, and farther inland, the tide and I, until we are come to those shallows where the salmon are at their mating—where the water is of such clarity the hand must touch it were the water to be known, and the depth is uncertain because of the great clearness of the current. There it will be, as like as not, the tide and I shall flush a brace of wood duck, the drake glorious; or a bevy of mergansers, and though there is a cabin within the mile it will be as it was when the land was young. Most agreeably and magically lonely, with a word thrown back from the near hills, and, but for this, only the voice of the shallows. And a grouse throating. If God is good to us, a mink may be sent to cross the stream before the boat—fluent as the water itself.

As wild, and as bright. And here, too, we will tarry for a time.

Have you been inland, along the river, to the sands where the deer have their crossing? At twilight and at dawn they come. Or when the moon is full, and the shadowy stealth of them is one with the shadows of the cedars, and the whiteness of their splashings is one with the wreath

about the rock. As furtive as the mists that rise and twist and droop in genuflection, and are gone. Have you been there? There is a bar where noon is drowsy with sun and the conversation of the stream.

Now when we have come to this place, the tide and its companions, we will know it for the place where the tide turns back, and there the boat will be beached and the fire lighted. And there coffee will be made, and the boughs spread. And yesterday shall seem as far removed as Cathay, time possessed and not possessing, and the hours leisurely and sufficient. It will be noon and drowsy with sun, and wakeful with the wind of the hills, and the sand shall creep out of the river to tell that the tide is turning.

I think that twilight never is truly twilight until one meets it in the hills and on a river. For at first the sun is red and pulsing as a rajah's jewel; and at the last the shadows pace like monks in somber habit. And always a single tall tree to westward, patient on the ridge of the world, is touched of flame. It is a presence and not a time, and the river is in and of it.

I think this would be a good place in which to bide a long, long while and hearken to the wisdom of the river. For so long a time that understanding should come of it—and dreams. This being accomplished one would wait a tide, and when the tide came one would go seaward with it.

AUTUMN

Autumn

The year pauses . . . dreams, and remembers

There is a swirling of small birds, like blown, brown leaves, over the hedges of the wild snowberry, and all the countryside is bemused with waiting. A brightness of leaves is drifting in the pasture ponds, and the calling of crows is tinctured with a questioning unrest. The spider-folk are voyaging on silken strands, where the wind wills, and the field mouse, secret from the searching hawk, goes earnestly about her harvest. The yield of the orchard stains the thirsty grass with crimson and treasure. And of mornings the mist comes inland from the river, and in the gentle grayness are the wings of waterfowl. Now all the countryside is waiting for some destined and near tomorrow.

How many a time have field and thicket, orchard and woodland waited as they wait now, while the year pauses and dreams and remembers. If but a score of seasons, encountered in one, might speak to us with the same voices—might multiply so the unidentified hungers, and awareness of change, of miracle, of a loveliness that has in it the nuance of the sad—no one might then endure. For the clerk would away from the ribbon counter, the builder from his walls and excavations, the farmer from his plow lands—to become again, as it was in the old days, footloose and wandering as any west wind. How many a time, when small birds were tossed above the snowberry, glinting and gone, and the silken floss of the spider went down the wind, and the trees dreamed wondrously toward the fall of the year, have men known the wonder and call of voices beloved, and denied, and accepted.

We dwell with the seasons, and make for them shrines all unperceived, for there is that in the blood—in the substance and mood of all things—that flows as a current of memory out of the past, declaring our kinship to each and all, great or minor; and even to trees that attire themselves gladly when it is autumn. The pagan poet within us stirs with the rousing seasons, and holds out his arms and entreats the mystery to tell us why that which is beautiful should wound so dearly. And never an answer comes, but only the cyclic seasons, and the tokens by which they are identified, and which tell off the years.

All of a kinship, quite all of them—the tree that waits in the pasture, the meadow mouse harvesting the ripening seed, the antlered deer in the canyon, the wild geese going over. All of a kinship. Quite all. For dear to each are the seasons, dear and prophetic; and if we shall say that the creatures and trees respond only to promptings they neither decree nor can fathom—what shall we say of ourselves, standing with something like prayer in our hearts where the cottonwoods shed a glow all about them, like softened, ineffable sunshine? Is this, too, an instinct? And if it be this, or even another marvel, a groping for understanding—what is it all but faith and a sure belief that partakes of religion?

Now of mornings, when the farm dogs are barking thinly and clear through the river mists, and the crows are questioning the day, and there is an odor of ripeness, of harvest, of the mellowing rich maturity of the year, we say only—one to another—that it is fall again, and the pastures need rain to refresh them. And it is strange, yet accustomed, that even the simplest of speech has meanings and comments that do not appear in words, yet are there so surely as though they were uttered. It is the fall of the year, and the pagan within us grieves for the Junes and Aprils that are forbidden to come again, and, yet grieving, stretches his arms toward the autumn and cries out in wonder. So it has always been.

We that welcome the seasons would keep them always, each turn of the year—would keep them, yet speed them; would have them always, yet with the marveling of children would run toward them, too. It is forbidden. We must wait as the trees. But when you have said of a tree that the very core and substance of it is in truth the record of its Aprils, wrought in its tissues, you may smile to think that we, too, keep the seasons with us. There are those who will say that their years are identified by the toils they have performed, or the lost endeavors once they

AUTUMN

dreamed; but in truth they are shaped of Aprils, successive Aprils, and summers that have been, and of autumns equal to these, and of winters that have awaited, each in its time, the coming of April again. So it is that they will remember, in the golden fall of the year—by the touch of the wind, or the play of sunshine on crimson leaves—sharply and dearly, how once they stood in a pathway of fallen leaves and marked the flight of a grouse, that rose in a swirl of crimson and gold. Far away and long ago. It is so that the seasons are kept, and in this wise only.

Belief in the seasons is faith; and the wonder they rouse is religion, and they are proof of the law. Is she not lovely to see, this strange, familiar one, crimson and golden with leaves, who tosses the restless flight of small brown birds above the wild hedges of snowberry?

Migration

Whistling wings in the twilight

At five, or such a matter, when the cottonwood shadows are lengthening swiftly, and cattle are loitering toward their barns, and crows have ceased their wild tumbling, and maybe a plover is calling across the green island—yes, around about five of an October afternoon—the wild ducks come driving in from northward. Then people with milk-pails stand to stare at them, and fishermen glance up from the sands beside the river, and a small boy over yonder forgets his errand. For the quiet air and the island sunset are filled with wings—with the whispering crispness of flight.

Where?

There! It will frost before morning. The ducks are coming in.

You look off toward the north country, high above the shore, to the flank of the sunset and the brightness that is before twilight. A freighter is making her way downriver, and the recurrent, even crashing of her waves wakes a tumult in the stillness. Presently, on a full tide, she will be with night and the ocean. You look away to the north, where a lone

AUTUMN

cloud is vagrant in the thoughtful sky—and minor and distant, tiny as millet seeds, swings the dark swiftness of the first flock. Undulant. Merging. Shaped to a crescent. Bladed as a spear. Thrown onward in a spaced and ordered dark crayon stroke of haste. Greater and even greater, with the breathless growth of approach.

Now wide as that horizon which the eye claims, and more swift than wind over water, and with a sound as of wind, the many flocks come thrusting in. Over the freighter in the sunset, above the broad and golden river, slanting down to the cottonwoods of the island, the green pasture, the rusty mullein, and the lakes that are burnished as a queen's mirror. And all the gathering twilight, through which the cattle pace so slowly, is vocal with the rush and whisper, the whistle and flutter, of a thousand homing wings.

Where?

There! Little and lost and grieving, as though the meadow mists had found a voice, you will hear plover crying. And evening has an island of her own.

Kindle a star for the late ones, above a pond in the lowlands, and let them shatter the whiteness of it as they curve down to the central water. Wings in the twilight over the island, lower and lower, out of the deepening north and the wraith of the sunset. You may not see them now. But they are near and guided. The river is whispering to herself in the stillness. The trees are vast and strange, the trees are mystery, against the darkening sky. There is a heron calling hoarsely. And a star is kindled.

Migration

Woodcutter Beside The River

Wild geese, and still a-coming!

Late Tuesday afternoon, near quitting time, a man named Hank—just Hank—was cutting wood at $1.50 a cord, and it was raining all the while, near Snag Point on the river. It seemed a long time since Hank had eaten his lunch, and both his feet were wet and cold. Not even cutting wood at $1.50 a cord will keep a man warm in a November rain storm when he needs new waterproof pants and coat, and new boots also, and can't see his way clear to afford them. But Hank did not realize that he felt miserable because he was used to it. A man hasn't any time to waste on feeling miserable when he is cutting wood, and the days are getting shorter, and he is planning on buying maybe a couple bottles Saturday.

Hank has a vocabulary of perhaps a few hundred words, and he can read a little. But a man doesn't need many words for to cut wood for a living, and he doesn't require reading when he has had his supper, because then he is ready to turn in, a man is, by God; because a man has to be up with the chickens, and down to Snag Point for to cut some more wood. It seems a natural and even a fortunate way of living—to Hank, as everybody calls him. Just Hank.

You take it, now, down around Snag Point, when the last few leaves are golden and sad, and it raining like that all day long, and the hour toward quitting time, and whether a man is limbing a tree or sawing a cut, with his feet wet, and his matches no good, he just thinks of his supper and getting his boots off. So Hank was thinking, with a good deal of concentration—for Hank—about his supper when he heard wild geese coming over the river. It's a favorite crossing for wild geese, at Snag Point.

Maybe Hank wouldn't have more than glanced up, while water ran down the back of his neck, for one flock of wild geese—a bunch, as Hank

calls it—for a man must keep on cutting wood. But the geese that crossed over the river late Tuesday afternoon, near quitting time, came in flock after flock, in multiple thousands; and the bright, far, wind-broken vagueness of their calling became a great voice, a music shouting down at Hank near Snag Point. A man was bound to look up, for a man won't see the like often, and Hank left his saw in the cut and looked up. He never had seen the beat of it.

Emotionally Hank is not complex, but still the stirring of an emotional impulse in Hank is emphatically an individual experience, a matter of wonder to him, and all the more so because Hank has no means of expressing it except by rudimentary profanity. When he saw how many geese there were, and heard the shining din of their high clamoring, he exclaimed aloud, and repeatedly, applying to himself the most profane and epithetical abuse of which he is capable. For Hank, gaping upward from the brush near Snag Point, was deeply moved to see and hear the exceeding wonder of the flight. He had no other words to praise it.

Hank wasn't hungry then, nor was he cold. He reckoned that the unbroken processional of wild geese, crossing the river, striving against the rainy wind, wavering, gleaming, and still a-coming, by God, must constitute an incalculable number. There must be a million of them geese. A million is an astronomical quantity to Hank. Of its true sum he has no notion. But to him it is the numerical ultimate. There must be a million of them geese.

Hank didn't mind the water squelching in his boots, for to him, watching the wild geese as they crossed the river, from grayness into grayness, his feet were wet no longer. He had been, he thought, yesterday in Alaska—somewhere up there, to northward—and he was going down to California, which is another place. And there wasn't any worry about going places, for the sky itself sustained him, and the level stroke of strong wings carried him lightly through the storm, whittling down the miles, by God, and all this to a yelping, a lot of talking, that had something of music in it—yes, something better than a band. A wild goose ain't cutting no wood at $1.50 a cord near Snag Point in the rain.

Hank knows what "free" means. It means something a man can get for nothing, if a man is lucky, like winning on a punchboard when you've had maybe a couple of beers and don't give a damn for a dollar. But "freedom" is a word Hank wouldn't know if you were to say it to him—and he had need of it late Tuesday afternoon, near quitting time, while he stared at the wonder of that flight. He phrased it in his mind. Wild geese, they ain't tied down. Wild geese been to Alaska yesterday. Tomorrow they will be in California. A man can't hardly realize it, so a man can't. All the while the water was running down the back of his neck, and now and then he would shake his head, to shed the gathering rain, but Hank was tranced by the geese.

It made him think, it glimpsed pictures, snatches of memory, of times when he was a boy. It made him think of running over fields. It made him think of long forgotten clouds. Hay in a wild meadow. Hazelnuts. A farm dog digging for a gopher. It made him think of these. But still the wild geese, and the wonder of them, were his central thought. The moment transcended every yesterday, and in it there were not any tomorrows. But still a man must cut wood again in the rain near Snag

Woodcutter Beside The River

67

Point come morning. And Hank came back from the flight lane, while the geese swept on.

It was so near to twilight, and the rain increasing, that Hank did not finish the cut. He drew out the saw—it needed setting again—and picked up his double-bitted axe and hid his wedges and maul, and still the wild geese were crossing the river out of grayness into grayness. There must have been a million of them. But Hank was cold and wet, and hungry. It was a hard way to serve the Lord.

"Now if I could-a knocked down maybe two-three of them geese—" mused Hank, going home from the river. He struggled then with a difficult thought. For it didn't seem right. And so Hank swore aloud as best he could, and dismissed it. He was thinking again of getting his boots off.

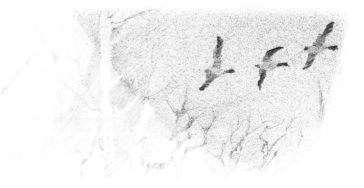

Five Teal In A Forest

Gently shattering the solitude

Five teal—and these almost are the smallest of wild ducks—were idling in the river where the near alders confer darkness upon the deep strength of the current. And from the alders, that stand among willows, the hills on either hand thrust swiftly upward to a remote and stainless sky, against which are set the fortunate trees that have sight forever of the ocean, and that taste of the timeless sea wind. The hills are clothed with fir, with cedar, and with spruce—and these last in their young verdure would seem to have retained the mists that visit the valley at morning. There were five teal at the bend of the river.

And because of the five there was no loneliness, and the darkness of the stream in late afternoon was brightened by the flash of a feather, the turn of a small and comely head, the lift and stroke of a wing. One will be certain to believe, who has known trees and rivers in their more than several moods, that they are capable of contriving and experiencing loneliness. For they seem sometimes to approach grief quite as we do, and to be engaged in meditations that depress them gently. The water listens for

AUTUMN

a voice it may not hear. The trees are all of a mute sadness. Is it a trick of light and shadow? And is it only that the mood is ours, responsive to those elder influences that are beyond logic?

No. The river at such a time and the still trees that watch—the very hills themselves—share in a common loneliness for life that moves and is free, that walks beside the river, or traces patterns of silver on its surface, or sunders the stillness with wings, or bends to the water for drink. And the five teal, setting their breasts to the flow of the river, ransomed even the mountains from a curious, brooding sorcery.

By means so modest as these the stream was encouraged and the hills comforted. For there is nothing quite so comforting in experience, so fraught with healing, so abundant of simple faith, as to be far in a lonely place and yet escape loneliness. This is an old and pagan comradeship. It is achieved for us by five waterfowl that lift from the river, beading the dark water as they rise—swerving, wheeling, rising midway of the misty spruces, until their wings make play of the sun through the forest. They have shattered solitude so gently that she is glad of heart. Five teal on the secret river, where the near alders confer darkness.

Give you good fortune always, small people of the river! A favoring wind and a path without falcons. Give you good fortune and a haven of whispering rushes, south and yet south of here, where naught shall creep toward you with evil, nor stand suddenly before you in a shape of fear.

And sweet water, and the pleasant savor of marshes that have always been, and mornings of grateful gray fog, and noons of drowsing on lakes all burnished—and white, strange nights of stars. Give you good fortune and a path without falcons always, small conquerors of solitude, and April again in her season.

Five Teal In A Forest

They were gone round the bend of the river.

A Tryst With October The Dancer

Stained leaves by the old logging road

A hunter, having kissed his wife, struck off across the farm lands for the hills, pausing only to make his dog go home at the pasture fence. He had a tryst with October, and he drank the air as though it had been new cider—which it seemed, in part. The hills lifted before him, and the sun blessed them where the cloud had passed, and on the hills the leaves were beginning to turn. In the meadow, as he went to the hills, the mushrooms were white astonishment, and the ground squirrels ranged far from their burrows.

AUTUMN

Late in the summer, cutting wood on the slope, he had seen the prints of the buck in the black earth of the brushy trail, and twice it had come to the wood lot at morning. Once it had stood a long moment to look back at him. His heart told him now that surely he should come upon the buck again, nor need a second shot. He entered the hills with a prayer in his heart to keep his tryst with October, the dancer.

The grouse in the stream bed, seeking gravel, the squirrel in the tree beneath which the strewn husks were bright, had no fear of him as he passed. In the pool at the ford, where the stream rested, the trout parr were rising, and the hunter drank from the pool—face down, he drank. And he gave praise as he drank, to the giver.

For the wonder and beauty of life, its completeness; the wonder and magic of life, sorcerous, changing; the wonder and dearness of life, that is like to an ache in the throat. For the comely face of the day, and the crystalline coolness of water so clear that the surface is touched before ever the surface is seen. For all this he gave praise to the giver.

It seemed to the hunter that in a glade to the west he came then upon October, with a coronal of scarlet and gold on her dusky hair, and with leaves for her garment, and these tinted with Autumn. October, the dancer of leaves. Her eyes were as brightly dark as the fruit of the wild vine, and brown of thigh was October in the glade as she danced, and on her lips was laughter. In the sunny, clear silence, almost he heard it. Yet at his coming she fled from the glade, and he crossed over, carefully then, to seek for the print of a deer's hooves where the spring seeped through the sword-fern. The hillside was imminent now. He felt the loom of the hill, the great nearness.

Where the buck had set his prints, beside the hill spring, the water yet was cloudy, the fern still bent. The hunter moved as a shadow moves, into the waiting wood—the quiet and watchful trees—and the little brown rabbit whirled and was gone. Over the hunter the high hawk hunted,

wheeling and turning. Quietly. Quietly then. In the silence of the forest, sunflecked, were voices of musical silence. The hunter stood to listen in the tranced stillness, and to breathe of the fern. And he said a prayer in his heart once more.

For the beauty and strangeness of life, all its changing rich pattern; the beauty and music of life, its voices and harmonies; the beauty and pity of life, its bending compassion. For the antlered deer that somewhere waited the pressure of a finger, the crack of a rifle. Go slowly now. Slowly. Listen. There was only the wind in the fir tops.

The cloud drift was over the sun, the shadow was over the sun-warm rock, and there fell through the stillness, hawk against cloud, a sprinkle of raindrops. Slowly. Go slowly.

Do you know the place near the head of the creek where a cliff lifts up at the right hand, and to the left there are traces of the old logging road? There are rock flowers on the sheer wall of the cliff, set in the crannies, and the wild aster blooms in the fringe of the road, and the vine maple burns by the roadside. It was there or nearby.

The hunter came as a shadow comes out of the forest, to stand as a shadow might wait by the trace of the road, and very slowly he turned, now this way, now that, in the musical stillness. And slowly, so slowly, the rifle rose to his shoulder, and leveled and was still for the space of a heartbeat. At the crack of the rifle the hawk veered aside, far above him, and the tall cliff gave the gunshot back to him, echoing. Stepping into the old logging road, the hunter paced off the distance.

The buck lay still beside the grass-grown wheel rut, sprawled in mute mimicry of the leap that never was made. It had been a far, clean shot. The mist-wet aster leaves beneath the antlered head were stained as the leaves of the vine maple when the year turns.

They were stained as the leaves of October the dancer.

The Time Of The Crows

Leaves of ebony and the savor of life

The fall of the year is the time of crows. A leaf must be tinted and a wild aster withered before the crows are truly happy. The year must make ready for her farewell, and look to southward in the sun-haze, and glance to northward where the mists are gathering, before crows really discover the savor of life. It is autumn that is the mother of the crows. And they cry out to the fall of the year, and fly to meet the season, and fly darkly back again, and all the clans gather as one clan. Strident. Joyous. Restless. Flashing. This is the time of the crows.

Blown about and away like leaves of ebony. Cawing. Calling. Making sport of the wind that upbears them. Rejoicing in flight and pursuit. Caw! Caw! The wind brings the cry of the crows thinly to you, and the wind loses the cry. The black ones are thrown sprawling against a cloud. They are tossed and buffeted. They are cast tumbling down to their trees. Down and shiningly down to the council trees of the crows, where-from the meadows are seen, the farmer in his field, the shepherd dog staring down the road, the glistening of metals, the herds and the flocks, the green and the golden countenance of the world. There the crows perch, the one clan of the crows. The leaves are ripening and the wind is fresh. From the council trees of the crows it is evident that she draws near and nearer—she who is the mother of crows, she who passes to and fro upon the world and ripens the leaves to harvest. Cry out to her, clan of the crows. Fly to her, dark ones. The crows are blown about and away like leaves of ebony.

You to the right wing, flying strongly, what do you know of fields beyond the sky-line? You to the left wing, beating against the wind, what do you know of forage far to the southward? Then you must fly as the old ones fly. Let the wind have its way with you—down and down

The Time Of The Crows

toward the pastures. Suffer the wind to make sport for you—up and up until the earth is little and distant. Now call to the wind and the weather, that all the world may know the crows are flocking. And men in their fields, in the fields they till for the crows, will look upward to you and think how wisely the crows determine their seasons. Flashing. Strident. Joyous. Yet in the wildness of the cry there should be something of grief—of grief so near to gladness, or gladness so mixed with grief—that all will marvel at the cawing of the crows. Calling. Cawing. The crows are calling to their season.

If you were going away somewhere—and you, and you—and the time was made ready, and the day drew near, and you knew in your heart that you would be happy—and this is an elder knowledge that has little to do with fact—wouldn't you cry out to the time of your going, and look forward toward it, with eagerness, to view the curve of the world at the place where the sky bends down? Spring is a season not to be sufficiently commended, and summer is uniformly excellent and desired. But the fall of the year is the time of the crows. And men in their fields, at the fall of the year, will be listening to the crows, will be watching the clans, while they wonder how it may be that a crow should know of her coming. They are blown like leaves of ebony, and all the clans are one clan. Cawing. Calling. Burnished against the cloud. Autumn is mother to all the crows.

All Such Sounds As These

Mellow music beyond our praising

The sound of wind in grave, tall trees, whose crests are in the sunshine while at their feet the fern is bright with shadow. Now such a sound as that will follow you wherever you may go, and will become a hunger. For though none may tell the meaning of the wind in the trees, yet it is a language that all interpret—the speech, softly, incessantly reiterant, of the wind in the trees.

And such a homely, common sound as the far barking of a dog across the country miles—mellowed to music by the distance. Or such another sound as the lowing of cattle along toward twilight, when the grove makes for itself a shadow on the pasture where the killdeer are calling. Now such a sound as the calling of the killdeer, neither joyful, nor sad, nor plaintive—but agreeable, with a nuance this side of melancholy, to the listener. Or such a sound as calling cattle. C-o-o, boss! C-o-o-o-, boss! C-o-o! Across some meadow where the mists are gathering. And all such sounds as these.

And I like—Mr. Quimby said—the gossip, better than bugles, of engine bells in train yards, after nightfall, when folk are coming home or going away, and there are welcomes and goodbyes, and the rich night, smelling of train-smoke, is vibrant and singularly emotional with the sound of engine bells, each with a different throat, blending, dwindling, rising. Now such a sound as that.

Or such a sound as that of an axe in the clearing, as you approach it, the thudding fall of the blade, the impact, to which there is mated the recollection of odors. The vibrant, crisp whine of the saw, stricken to music, where men are cutting wood in the clearing, and there is a fragrance of fibers newly riven, of fronds underfoot, of resinous wounds. And all such homely, familiar, yet astonishingly memorable sounds as those of the axe and the saw.

Have you heard birds at morning, the half of an hour before sunrise, when they awaken? Very sleepily they begin the praise of creation and of the creator, and dawn comes out of the mystery that was night, and the sky is made to seem an awakening wonder while these voices take up the praise of the giver. Sometimes you have heard the grouse in the shadowy forest, with a sound like the beating of a great heart, or on the prairie with a sound like that of a drum—if the sound of a drum might be beautiful. Have you ever forgotten?

Who has heard the conversations of water, the whisper of lakes, the beat and thunder of the sea, the laughter and shouting of rivers, without remembering for so long as he is given to memory? These are agreeable sounds. They touch the heart with a hand primordial. They are timeless and yet they belong to the beginnings. Song across water, if heaven is good to the listener; or the spaced creaking of oars when at midnight the nets are lifted, and the fishermen count their catch while the ceaseless and meditative river repeats its message, for which there is not any interpreter, nor any is needed, over and over. These are sounds quite beyond our praising.

All Such Sounds As These

Now I—said Mr. Quimby—have been given to hear the rain on the roof when, as it happened, I imagined my trouble was great. Now there is a sound. It is a sound that comes slowly into the consciousness, and pervades it, and it is a sound somewhat comparable, in its effect, to cool fingers on the eyelids, and to a voice, well remembered and wordless, that speaks comfort. To a voice that whispers of healing. How many a time—observed Mr. Quimby—has the rain on the roof whispered to me until I became almost a child again, and it seemed I was, or readily might be, without care. It is a fancy. But half of life is in the fancy of us—half of life, or more than this. I incline—said Mr. Quimby—to the rain on the roof.

And all such sounds as these: The cry of a hunting hawk, slowly wheeling; the opening and shutting of doors in a frosty stillness; the whistles of river boats that have a hoarse wonder and sorcery all of their

AUTUMN

own; the cawing of crows when the cottonwoods are golden and vague through the mist; the distant laughter of children in their excitement, their laughter and all but indistinguishable words; the hollow rumbling of wheels on a wooden bridge; the rush and winnowing of mallard wings as the flock comes in to the river. Such sounds as these.

I remember—said Mr. Quimby—how once in the stillness, sudden and sweet and sad, without sadness, at a time when I had gone for the cattle, the plover were everywhere calling. Calling. To right and to left, behind and before, the plover were calling, and the sun was a great coin over the marshes, and the sunset thrust at the whispering rushes with a red lance. I remember the calling of the plover—and all such sounds as that.

They Took Him Beyond The Mountains

A dog to remember in October

On such a day as this—so ran his thoughts—the old dog went away never to come back. There is the very same savor in the air as when the kitchen door was opened, and that's what makes an autumn day sometimes the least bit sad. It was just such a day as this—he thought—it was fall, and the old dog loved the fall of the year, the way some dogs always do. Now such a day as this made him feel like a pup again, it really seemed to. He would have come back if he could, but somehow he didn't. And we never saw hide nor hair of him again.

We went out and hunted for him all through October, through leaf and vine and corn patch, along the country roads, through the pastures where he leaped when he had startled a pheasant, but it wasn't no manner of use. We called, but there was some sort of distance between us—a ditch that he couldn't leap. We called through October. The old dog never came back.

Some people say that he must have been taken somewhere beyond the mountains, for he was a dog to catch the eye of a thief. But that would be ten years or more ago, and he wasn't a young dog then. If they took him beyond the mountains they must have broken his heart, however good they were to him. They would want to take him maybe where the cattle were, but they couldn't comfort him with cattle. They must have broken his heart.

On such a day as this he liked to stand where the wind lifted his white ruff and stroked the flowing plume of his tail—and all the gold of him then would be bright in the sunshine, and his slim head would be lifted, and when he turned his head to you there would be gladness and laughter in his eyes. And back of his eyes lived someone who was honest, and brave and fond, with the ready wit for a jest and a heart that was quick to grief. I wonder—he thought—if they broke his heart over yonder across the mountains.

We used to walk in October, the two of us often, and to see him run with the wind was something of the beauty and gladness of life—he ran so cleanly and well and with such joyousness, leaping into the wind with the cool taste of it far in his throat. And when he came back to my side—so it was remembered—he had a glance for me that was blended of drollness and fondness, as though he were saying, over and over, "We two; we two!" He made a picture on a hill of October, with the wind in his ruff; and here it is etched.

He would be an old, old dog now, for he was not a young dog then.

But it is foolish—he thought—to think of him now as an old dog. That was ten years ago. And they broke his heart probably over beyond the mountains, and that was an end of that.

The little dogs gave him much laughter. He always thought they were funny, "Look," he would say, with his lip lifted, his eyes dancing, "share him with me! Isn't he a funny little ridiculous dog? Doesn't he amuse you, too?" Gentle and laughing and brave. For the big dogs that carried the fight to him, he had a flashing, lambent savagery, too swift for the eye to follow; the white fangs gleaming, slashing, gripping, and the warm eyes frosty with fury. But when the fight was at an end, and the old dog torn and tense, with the taut trembling of his passion still on him, what then but laughter! A joyous laughter in his eyes. Like that line from an old and half-remembered verse—"for laughter, with sword and steely harness, stood up at his side."

They may have taken him to the cattle country, but though he liked cattle with an instinct deep in his veins, they never could comfort him with cattle. A herd of dairy cows grazing, those times we walked in the country, and up went the fine head with its tapering muzzle and his gaze sparkled with animation. There was something about a herd that called to him, that is true, and it wasn't a primitive purpose to pursue—it was something else, something woven in the fine fiber of the old dog. Yet though they took him beyond the mountains they must have found that they couldn't comfort him with cattle. There was a leash on him still, you comprehend, and it must have drawn at him until his heart was broken.

Well—so his thought ran—anyhow it is something to have had the old dog for a friend. For it was friendship, and it honored me. It made me humble sometimes by the fond and honest quality of it. This mind so unlike ours, and yet so like to ours, it was in some ways much the finer mind. This spirit, rather, in its simplicity and truth, its fond fidelity. On such a day as this the old dog went away, nor hide nor hair of him they ever saw again.

They Took Him Beyond The Mountains

And is it sentimentality somehow to fancy now that, since he neither is here nor yet beyond the mountains—for he was an old dog even then—he must be with October on some hill of hers? Then call it so if call it so you must. This much is truth, at least—he thought—that you have never had a dog such as he was, or you would understand. He runs now with October, through the scarlet vine and brier, and golden drift of leaves, and is not far away. Time and mischance have no authority in this. Surely the old dog is running with October, with happiness in his heart and laughter in his eyes, to start a pheasant such as we have never seen, to have the wind of such a rabbit as is all of desire. This essence we call life, they cannot quench it when they take it, as they will, beyond the mountains. The old dog isn't far away.

I had a good dog once—so ran his thought—and such a day as this it was, an October morning, when he went away. I had a good dog once and so I have him yet.

WINTER

Storm On The River

Wild and boisterous, squandering splendor

One of the disadvantages of living in a city, as a kind of captive who is away on good-conduct leave not more than occasionally, is that city folks seldom see the tremendous but not unforbidding face of the storm. They say to each other, when the wind has its stride and rain falls peltingly, when flowers bend and vines clash against the wall, "Well, it is storming again." And having made this comment, they very sensibly defy the storm, with walls the carpenter built or the mason reared, or at most they venture so far as the grocery store. And, taking it all in all, one thing with another, their walls, their streets, their companion dwellings, their office buildings and their closed cars, they know less about the actual countenance of the storm than does the field mouse which scurries for its grass tufts when the first drop makes a fearsome crater in the sand beside the stream.

But the wide Columbia, with a white stern-wheeler nosing out from behind Government Island, is a grand place for storm. There the storm has distance for its stride, and trees to bend before it and water to toss and whip to spray, and various birds that may or must be driven, singly or in flocks, against a windy, rolling sky. The river is a proper place for storm. There falls a silence on the stream, a truce of minor sounds: a silence so pervasive and far thrown that the stream, and the shore, and the tall, slim cottonwoods, seem conspirators in silence, and somewhat awed, and surely waiting. They are waiting for storm. So hushed. So queerly vigilant. So certain of that which must befall.

In advance of storm on the river comes sorcery, a matter of moody yet matchless harmony in color, so that the waiting silence shall be strange of hue; and sand nor water, tree nor ship, may seem that for the fittings of an afternoon late in the year. The hills are purple as with deep Tyrian dyes, and the slim, tall cottonwoods of the island are yellow as treasure. The sandbar has the hue of fractured steel, and now our steamer, well beyond the island, is of the whiteness of a gull's breast; a whiteness difficult to look upon. And from her stack the spire of smoke stands stiffly in the brooding air. But the river's self is lune-green, luminous, and over the vastness of the flow has fallen a light comparable to the tint of the cottonwood leaves, but which is thinly diffused and somewhat as an old memory, evasive, sweetly sad.

A mist walks up the river, and of a sudden the far cottonwoods toss and sway beneath a frowning onward cloud, and the mist is distant rain, thrusting a water wreath before it. And this is storm. Waves wake to shatter the moon color of the current, until the breast of the river is flecked with ermine, and the water gives tongue. Now storm overtakes the stern-wheeler, white as the breast of a gull, and she is invisible within it for the space of moments; is glimpsed, is lost, is seen again. There are crows cawing before the wind, and they flee not without a certain joyousness; wind-tossed, thrust down, borne upward, carried like black drift in the lofty currents, and calling one to another. But the wild ducks cling close to the breast of the river, flying almost with their wingtips in the waves—though they drive against the storm, piercing it to its gray heart, and so are gone. Now it is nearer, wilder, infinitely beautiful, and rain comes lancing down, and the near trees are swaying. And of a moment all is the monotone of the rain—cottonwoods, sandbar, steamer, stream and cloud, all of a kindred grayness, all converts and thralls to storm. It is raining heavily, methodically, as though in the advance it had squandered enough of splendor.

Storm On The River

We are too snug within our houses. Towns and cities hold us prisoner, and with our comfortable consent. Almost we have forgotten the sheen of rain on a green, wild leaf, and that leaf multitudinously multiplied. We withdraw from the moods of nature, and speak often of fine days, as though fine days were few. Sir, it must needs be a rough day, indeed, wild and boisterous, that is not fine to see, and in which it is not agreeable to be abroad.

Sometime, between symphonies and picture shows, you should see for yourself how storm comes up the river.

WINTER

A Jaybird In January

Mockery by a jaunty rogue

Wet and windy weather, wild and rainy weather, with Drift creek coming up fast and the wine-stained alders striving in the gusty seawind. But a crested jaybird on an alder bough, peering down to see the swirling, saffron stream, what need a jaybird care? Come storm or sunshine, January or June, it is all one to a jaybird, for joyousness is a matter of being alive. And the shrouded storm swept over the creek in gray processional, while the jaybird mocked the storm. Yes, sir, she was coming up pretty fast.

Those that have a crest to wear should bear it jauntily. And those that have a jaybird's heart should never know a piety. Fear is for lesser fowl and greater ones. Let the storm strike chillness to them in the wine-stained alder thickets all along the creek. Let them hide away. For they haven't the secret that jaybirds possess, the intuition that is the key to all manner of things, which is that wet and windy weather, any sort of weather, scarcely can be otherwise than good weather, too. From his bough in the striving alder, the jaybird peered at the yellow water. On a jaybird's word, mister, she's coming up fast. And out of a glad and whimsical heart, the heart of a rogue with a jaunty crest, the jaybird mocked the rain.

You fly through the gusty, dim smother of it—so—and away, if you are a jaybird, well knowing that never a wittier, wiser, more daring, thievish and excellent fellow ever came from the egg into an excellent world, and the alders across the creek receive you—so—and then you fly back again, mocking the wind and the wetness. And fishermen, chill at their fire, tormented of wind and of patience, cannot but admire you—by a saffron, dignified eddy of Drift creek not far from the sea. You have such an admirable mocking, fine humor for all sorts of weather—as though the manner of day did not matter. The jaybird dined as he perched on the bough of the alder, and peered at the hastening current again. Old creek was coming up pretty fast.

This is a jaybird's world in the wet, wild winter weather, for a jaybird doesn't mind it, and he bears his crest bravely to meet it, and mockery is in his remarks, as though the weather were sunny. And the wind and the rain that swirl grayly around him, these are a jaybird's privilege, too. It is a whimsical, droll business to be alive, he was remarking, and one should not expect too greatly of it, and yet it is always a happy affair, if you consider it quite as a jaybird should. They that wear crests ought to know how to bear them. Jauntily. So. And the jaybird peered down the creek again, to perceive that a jaybird had been entirely correct in a jay-bird's conclusions. She was coming up fast in an early wild twilight.

Jim Dinkens of Beagle, he says that eagles won't touch 'em.

A Jaybird In January

Gale On The Coast

Frothing sands . . . and a forest of driftwood

The wind came in the night, rushing irresistibly out of the south-western ocean, and in the loud grayness of dawn the towering great seas advanced upon the beaches and bird rocks, the stout headlands, to strike in thunderous surf that was dissolved into a violent whiteness. The land trembled. It is repayment to wait for such a surf and such a scene, the half of a lifetime. How suited to storm is our mother the ocean, whose strength is destructive, creative, vastly incalculable. People stood in the rain and the smother, breasting the wind, to watch with awe that is near to prayer, while of wind and sea were contrived—somehow—a memory. For this wildness, this freedom, the gigantic impetuosity and anger of the sea, seemed somehow to have been remembered, to have been lived before—far away and long ago—on another headland. She is our mother the sea.

Now the sea-fowl were tossed in the spindrift, where the combers were creaming, and the gulls would appear to have a wild gladness in the vigor of the gale, while the midget sandpipers were in nowise afraid, but kept their formation above the frothing sands, where the drift logs were tossing and twirling. But the small phalarope birds, that in fair weather are to be found cruising the tide rips long miles offshore, were carried inland into the alien forest or by great good fortune found wayside pools that were secure from the constant wind. But what weather shall distress the sea gull? He hovered the loudness of it on pliant wing, swerved and was swept away, rose curvingly and was restored to his vantage in the full flow of the gale. The wild geese went laboring by, low to that terrible water. It would be high tide at noon.

She gathers the massive drift, the great logs that have escaped the mill, the trees that descended in freshet, and batters the dune and the cliff beyond the farthest advances of all tides that are remembered. Of such strength and blind purpose was the beginning of the world. So the ocean, as the morning drew on toward noon, the wind unabating, ceaselessly hurled a forest of driftwood against rock and seawall—and the spume blossomed whitely at a height that obscured the rock itself, and

fell as it had lifted in shuddering thunder tone. There was deity yonder.
Religion. Out yonder oddly enough, where stormy wind and wild sea
made their own false evening. In such a mood the sea needs no interpreter.

"It will blow itself out," the people said, standing yet to watch.
Then all the pastures were flooded with the great tide, and river and

creek were broadened incredibly far beyond their bridges, and the fugitive drift, twirling and turning in the strong inland flow of the streams, found often its haven where yesterday the cattle were grazing. The tall rain moved processionally over the silver meadow. It was noon and high tide. They looked wonderingly one at another, while imperceptibly for the time, but surely, the tumult lessened and the sea withdrew. The wind was lively then, but less, and very gradually the shore ceased to tremble. The day drew on toward a rainy twilight.

New Snow

Perfection, with a curious fragrance

Human artists may strive for perfection, but there is no masterpiece, perhaps, that does not lack for something in the eye of its producer. But a field of snow new fallen in a country kind of place, the immaculate white silence of it yet unmarred, almost contrives perfection. The windless air is sweetly chill, with the curious fragrance—itself an absence of odor—which is the breath of the snow. And from the back stoop to the pasture fence, and so to the hazel thicket, and the forested hill beyond, is that white silence, that wintry completeness, so like an exclamation.

The snow would seem to flow, thus arrested, with the undulant surface of earth. It has neglected nothing. Each fence post is capped with snow, and the woodpile is a study in forgiven and softened angularity. There are white mysteries hither and yonder. And all the motionless hazel is burdened with the stainless beauty of it, while under the hazel are purple shadows that deepen into the shade. Now if it so chances that there is sun on the snow, the new snow, from the back porch to the oak on the hill, the silence of the snow will be radiant as shouting. No sound. No track to mar it. Just snow. Another of the commonplaces of nature that approach perfection.

But the juncos will be abroad very presently, and they will scatter the snow from the weed stalk—as is their lawful right. At night, the field mice, creeping along the fences, will leave little-small footprints in token of the courage of field mice. And when the moon is risen, to walk with long golden strides through a thinness of cloud, the wild woods rabbits will come forth from the hazel to dance on the snow. The snow will be beginning to wear out, which of itself is really a cheerful absurdity. Over and over again, endlessly repeating.

WINTER

Snow Is For Country Places

A breathless white silence

It should never snow in towns, for they cannot appreciate snow, except in the farthest suburbs. It is a fabric for the attiring of fields and fir trees, at some distance from streets and highways, where there is little to mar it. Perhaps the track of a rabbit. Or the elfin footprints of meadow mice. Or where juncos have thronged about a brown weed stalk. And there's the stride of a tall cock pheasant. But it never should snow in towns.

In towns the snow will be sullied so soon as it is fallen—by foot and wheel, and the casual wastes of the city. The spinning, soft fall of the snow, that drifts by the windows, and rests for a moment on furs, this visiting whiteness of silence, cannot come to the street without scathe. It wants hills, does the snow, and wide grass lands, and alders alongside of rivers. So it is that people in towns, when it is snowing, will think of the country. They won't be thinking of towns. The snow is for country places.

At the time of snow in towns, when nothing has patience to leave the snow as it should be, untrodden, unbroken, you might look from the porch of a farm to see the white gloom of the mountains that are seaward, or a pasture that's all a white stillness—quite perfect. And, so looking, it must seem that you know something not to be uttered, since it lacks words to shape it; something kindred to all desire, and yet silenced. So it would seem from a farm window.

Snow is for country places, and rivers, and ranges of hills, and turf that needs healing. If you were yonder, away through the veil of it, you would come upon a river running darkly through the snow, the rocks and clay of its bank hidden in whiteness, and the stream sharply defined, and more vital than ever, yet thrice as secret. You would chance upon meadows breathless with a white silence, and upon trees whose branches are bending to bear the snow of the foothills; and shrouded willow and maple, and the white, wonderful lift of the slope that rises smoothly until it is lost in the snowfall. All strange, all changed. And whitely arrested by the strangeness and wonder of snow.

There would be an odor and fragrance of snow, and through the weave of the storm a flight of birds, rising, falling, lost in the silence. This is a continent in itself, and unpeopled. There is none near you—and you alone in the whiteness that cannot have border nor province. And the great flakes spinning slowly.

Snow is for country places.

Snow Is For Country Places

A Christmas Reverie

From out where the stars are . . .

Something came into town last night from out where the stars are
blinking in blue space. You could not see it nor hear it nor touch it with
quick hands—for it is more gossamer than any cloud, more elusive than
any star beam, and yet it has the strength of steel and the constancy of
life. It is intangible yet actual, ephemeral yet enduring, and in it is the will
of the tides, the purity of the wind, the patient vigor of that purpose
which shaped the world and tossed it whirling into space. Something
came into town.

Merry Christmas!

With what effect it whispers to us, so that each one, be he milkman
or millionaire, finds true fraternity in his heart this morning, and issues
from his domicile to cry a greeting to friend and stranger. There is mist
in the purple valley. Bracken and conifer are heavy with dampness, nun-
gray with the mist that cloaks them. Winter in the country, and the sun
breaking through. A crow to westward, calling and dolor in the call.
Crow, it is your misfortune to be a bird this day. Black jackanapes, never

to know Christmas! This singular sense of well being, this lightness, this light that breaks in upon us—and what may it mean, sir? Why, as to that, it means no more than this: it is good to rejoice, to be clean of purpose, to be again as children. And a great wave of sun-tipped laughter running round the planet.

Memory, come here; let us sit by the fire together. Was ever such candy as the striped sticks of yore? Was ever toy so marvelous as the cast-iron train with wheels that would not turn? Was ever book so thumbed in after years, so loved, so quoted of strange incident as "The Swiss Family Robinson"? And, bless my soul, here is a popcorn ball, sticking a trifle . . . but, no matter. Deep down in the toe, beyond the last fugitive hazelnut, what might that be? It is huge, it is round, it is mysterious. An orange, as golden as the fruit of fair Hesperides! A veritable orange, smelling wondrously of the south. Can you equal that for Christmas?

Merry Christmas!

Yesterday an enmity was important. Nay, it controlled one. And yesterday there were great plans of commerce, which, if not pressed successfully to conclusion, must mar the closing year with black regrets. This is passing strange. How far away our yesterday has drifted overnight, how unimportant and unreal it seems; how reedlike the faint, piping voice of its requirements. Not a bad fellow at heart. Foolish to feed a grudge. As for the other, it must wait, since this is not the time to think of it. An ember falling on the hearth, a fat flame dancing upward . . . what a cheerful clamor children make on Christmas Day!

Essentially a day for children. No doubt of it. It is true they expect more than children used to expect. Still it is little enough. Cannot be children always, you know. Must laugh and be merry while they may. Dollar or two more or less. In a few years, in a surprisingly short space of time, they will have grown up, and laughter will not come so readily to them, nor trifles have the sheen and beauty of treasures. Then they will wait for Christmas, look forward to it, hunger for it, for quite another reason. Indeed, they shall. For it shall bring their lost childhood back to them, out of the unrelenting years that yield to no other key. What is more precious than laughter—than laughter without a trace of tiredness in it, or of malice, or of worldly wisdom? Laughter that yields its full quota of happiness; that is naught else? Ah, that's a deep one! Fiddlesticks. Nothing is more precious than laughter. The laughter of children.

Day that He was born. There is an immaterial controversy about that. Matter of opinion, say some; matter of record, say others. Controversy. Forever bickering over immaterial matters, mere niceties of meticulous fact. Why, sir, that He was born is the fact that rises brightly above all others, up and up like the sun's self, driving away the quarrelsome creeds, drying the tears of the race, banishing all shadows—presaging a better day. And is this not the morning of His birth? What proof have you contrariwise? It is lovely enough, and kind enough, and generous enough, to be His own—since He was all this and more. We ask too many questions that are pointless and seek too many goals that are not worth the seeking. They have tangled us tightly in doctrine. But we are breaking loose . . . and these treasured teachings shall endure. Have no doubt of that.

A Christmas Reverie

Something came into town last night, from out where the stars are. It has made the city and the world far better to be in, far better to dwell in—it has made and is making. You could not escape it if you would. For it enters hearts and bides there. There is a nun-gray mist in the valley, but no mist is in the home.

Merry Christmas you say?

Merry Christmas to you!